100 Questions and Answers About Americans

Michigan State University School of Journalism

Read The Spirit Books

an imprint of
David Crumm Media, LLC
Canton, Michigan

For more information and further discussion, visit

http://news.jrn.msu.edu/culturalcompetence

Cover art and design by
Rick Nease
www.RickNeaseArt.com

Published By
Read The Spirit Books
an imprint of
David Crumm Media, LLC
42015 Ford Rd., Suite 234
Canton, Michigan, USA

For information about customized editions, bulk purchases
or permissions, contact David Crumm Media, LLC at info@
DavidCrummMedia.com

Contents

About This Guide

MICHIGAN STATE UNIVERSITY journalism students and faculty created this guide to help individuals from abroad understand American customs and behaviors.

We began by asking international students for questions they had about America and Americans. We learned that perceptions of Americans are very different from one person or culture to the next. After whittling the questions down to 100 that we thought were best, we placed the questions into categories such as social behavior, education and race. We then researched the questions and consulted with experts. The result? This guide, which uses studies and surveys, generalities and ranges of possibilities to explain U.S. culture.

Not all parts of the United States are alike — and neither are all Americans. There can be greater differences within one country than there are between two countries. Even brothers and sisters from the same family can be quite different.

Although this guide explores differences, we discovered that similarities are far more common. We all want to understand and to be understood, to be accepted and to grow. We want to be secure and to be fulfilled. We want to be respected.

After you read "100 Questions and Answers About Americans," start having deeper conversations on your own. Each person you talk to can tell you about their own experience, but their experience is not the same as someone else's. So, talk to many people. Ask them about what you read in this guide. Tell them about yourself. You are an ambassador of your country and might find yourself answering 100 questions about your homeland.

* * *

Thank you to the people from Africa, Europe, Asia, Australia, North and South America who provided us with questions.

Individuals from several Michigan State University departments helped produce this guide, which was funded by a Creating Inclusive Excellence Grant from the Office for Inclusion and Intercultural Initiatives. They include:

Paulette Granberry Russell, senior advisor to the president for diversity, and director of the MSU Office for Inclusion and Intercultural Initiatives, who proposed this subject

D. Venice Smith, consultant for multicultural issues, education and development, MSU Office for Inclusion and Intercultural Initiatives

Peter Briggs, director of the MSU Office for International Students and Scholars

Joy Walter, international student advisor/community outreach coordinator, OISS

Bess Carey, MSU Office of Study Abroad

Kathy M. Collins, director of MSU Residence Education and Housing Services and Eduardo Olivo of the Residence Education Team

Lawrence Zwier, associate director of curriculum at the MSU English Language Center

Patricia Walters, associate director and student advisor at the MSU English Language Center

Geraldine Alumit Zeldes, associate professor, MSU School of Journalism

John Golaszewski, director, Business & Community Affairs at the Michigan Department of Civil Rights

The authors are MSU students Michelle Armstead, Gabrielle Austin, Celeste Bott, Marlee Delaney, Stephanie Dippoliti, Max Gun, Emily Jaslove, Aaron Jordan, Alexandra McNeill, Katherine Miller, Ashiyr Pierson, Marissa Russo, Merinda Valley, Jessica Warfield, Jasmine Watts and Danielle Woodward.

— *Joe Grimm, visiting editor in residence, MSU School of Journalism*

Foreword

PEOPLE ACROSS THE world are interacting with an increased frequency that makes understanding our respective cultural ways more important than ever. Building a global workforce, working to resolve global challenges and reducing the risk of international conflicts all demand people with a comfort zone that is not limited by their cultural boundaries.

International enrollment at U.S. universities continues to rise, and this presents wonderful opportunities for cross-cultural engagement. This guide plays a helpful, practical and important role in helping international students understand some basics of U.S. culture and stimulate the deeper introspection we all need to be good global citizens.

— Peter Briggs, director, Office for International Students and Scholars, Michigan State University

General

1. Americans seem to be proud of their country. Is this true?

Yes. Americans are generally proud of their country, its values and freedoms. Several holidays such as Independence Day (the Fourth of July) celebrate the United States' history. Recent tragedies such as terror attacks and natural disasters unite the country and evoke feelings of patriotism.

2. How big is the United States?

The United States covers 3.794 million square miles, or 9.827 million square kilometers, which makes it the world's third largest country after Russia and Canada. The United States has 50 states, Washington, D.C., where the federal government is located, and nine territories. The United States is the third most populous country in the world after China and India. The population reached 317 million in 2013 and is growing by one person every 14 seconds.

3. Is America culturally diverse?

The 2010 U.S. Census identified 21 ancestry groups that had 2.5 million or more people in each. The largest groups reported ancestry in Germany, Ireland, Mexico, England and Africa. The United States has historically promoted itself as a haven for immigrants. Most American families came here from other countries, often as part of large migrations. Additionally, a core American value, as described by Wayne Baker's 2013 book, "United America," is respect for others. He wrote, "More than 90 percent of Americans in the national surveys I conducted said that respect for people of different racial and ethnic groups is important to them."

4. How culturally aware are Americans?

Although this country contains many cultures, the news media and educational systems focus on the United States and do not look abroad as much as some other countries do. Many organizations and campaigns in the United States promote cultural awareness. These tend to focus on awareness of cultures as practiced within the country. Awareness, like cultural background, can vary widely among Americans.

5. Americans seem to be very welcoming. Is that true throughout the United States?

It is not easy to generalize behaviors in any country. Although many Americans seem outgoing and welcoming, this is not always true. Mannerisms can be different according to regions in the United States and according to the person. The Midwest has a reputation for being friendlier than some other regions, but that is not universally true. This impression is also influenced by whom you've met.

6. Why do Americans make a big deal out of someone being international?

Although the United States has people from all over the world, Americans still find other cultures interesting. Many Americans will lose their culture and traditions as new generations of their family are born. They become accustomed to the "American lifestyle." When meeting people with strong ties to their culture, Americans are generally curious to learn more about them and their traditions.

7. Do Americans want to be friends with people from other countries?

Americans are generally open to becoming friends with people of different nationalities. Many Americans travel and are used to meeting people from other places who have come to the United States. This interest can lead to friendship or to a more casual acquaintance.

8. How informed are Americans about the world?

This varies, but in general Americans know less about the world compared to citizens of many other nations. The World Savvy Global Competency Poll found that 74 percent of 18- to 24-year-olds wish that high school classes taught them more about the world. Only 38 percent of students felt that world events were regularly discussed in their high school classroom. Overall, Americans do not score well on world geography exams.

9. What matters more, laws or leaders?

The U.S. justice system is based on "the rule of law." Regulations, passed by elected bodies, have more power than the people who enforce the laws. If people who enforce the laws abuse their positions, they can be removed.

Social Behavior

10. People in the United States smile at strangers for no reason. Why is that and what is the meaning?

Many Americans smile at people to be friendly. It is the same reason some people say hello to strangers. To Americans, being friendly is not the same as being a friend. An American might give a friendly greeting to someone they do not even know on one day and not remember that person the next day. Friendships are relationships built over time. The smiles and greetings do mean, however, that you are in an environment where friendship is possible.

11. How do I respond to "Have a nice day!" or "How are you?" or "How's it going?"

These are ways to greet people, even strangers. You could respond to "Have a nice day," by saying, "You, too." or "Thanks." "How are you?" and "How's it going?" is like saying "Hello." Appropriate responses are "fine," "good," "great" or "OK." Americans generally do not mean these as sincere questions about someone's health or happiness.

12. What are appropriate ways to greet people in the United States?

"Hello" or "How are you?" or "It's nice to meet you," often are enough. First-time acquaintances or individuals meeting in professional situations typically shake hands, and many females greet their friends with a hug. There are no widespread U.S. customs about males and females greeting as there are in some cultures.

13. How are apologies given and received?

Apologies are generally given when you have done something wrong, inconvenienced someone, startled them or upset them. This could be something as small as bumping into someone or stepping on someone's foot. Responses to an apology include, "No, you're fine," "It's OK," and "Don't worry about it."

14. How do I make American friends?

Take the first step by introducing yourself. To build relationships, it is important to connect with the person. In America, that means finding something in common to talk about or do together. Start a conversation with a person to get to know them. Working in an organization, on a team or on a class project can give you a shared interest and something in common.

15. How can I connect with people here if I don't understand cultural things like old TV shows, celebrities or sports?

Americans most often form friendships with people who have similar interests and experiences. You can become friends with Americans even if you don't understand cultural references. To start a conversation, speak generally. Asking a person a question and then listening to their answer can help you understand their interests and personality.

Here are several conversation starters to try:

What is your major?
What is your year in school?
Where are you from?

You can also start talking about something going on in class, an event on campus or a topic in the news that isn't controversial. Even sharing perspectives can be a way to connect. Keep in mind that despite cultural and language differences, people have a lot in common.

16. How much personal space should I maintain between others and myself when speaking to them or riding the bus?

Preferences vary. An American anthropologist found that Americans are comfortable with five to 10 feet (1.5 to 3 meters) between themselves and strangers. Friends and family often interact at about half that distance. When speaking with someone, pay attention to his or her body language. If they step back, this might mean they want more space. If they move closer, they might prefer a shorter distance. Mirror the other person's behavior, and let them determine the space between you.

17. What are American customs for eye contact?

In the United States, eye contact is regarded as a sign of respect and attentiveness. When speaking to someone or being spoken to, look them in the eye. Constantly looking away from a person during a conversation can imply disinterest, dishonesty or a lack of self-confidence. However, most Americans find constant eye contact to be uncomfortable and avoid it. As you would do with personal space, watch the other person for signs and mirror them. Though direct eye contact might be taken as a sign of disrespect in some cultures, it is not seen that way in America.

18. What does holding hands mean in America?

This usually means that the people have a romantic involvement, unless it is an adult holding a child's hand. Americans tend not to hold hands or link arms with friends or relatives, as people in some cultures do. Some Americans also hold hands for comfort when frightened.

19. When should I tip and how much should I leave?

It is customary, but not mandatory, to tip service workers with money in addition to the bill and taxes. In restaurants where food is brought to the table, tips or a gratuity are the majority of a worker's pay. The amount is a percentage of the pre-tax bill and is based on the quality of service. Ten percent recognizes adequate service, 15 percent is for good service and 20 percent implies excellent service. Leaving no tip or a very small one can be seen as an insult or a complaint. Some restaurants, especially for large parties, will add a gratuity to the bill.

Tipping guidelines

Waiters in sit-down restaurants	5-20 percent
Food deliveries	As above, $2 minimum
Baggage handler	$1 per bag
Bartender	$1-2 per drink
Car parker	$1-2
Coat check	$1 per coat if free
Coffee place with tip jar	Optional
Grocery bagger	None
Taxi/limo driver	10-15 percent
Bus driver	None
Haircuts	15-20 percent
Hotel maid	$1-2 per night

Education

21. How does a typical college classroom function in the United States?

It is common for professors to strive for collaboration. Professors encourage participation, especially when it comes to sharing experiences and opinions. Students benefit and learn from their peers. The smaller the class or meeting, the more participation is encouraged and may help a student's grade. In many courses, expect group projects, presentations in front of the class and assignments that provide hands-on or in-the-field experience.

22. Why is it acceptable for students to speak out and challenge professors?

In American colleges, the relationship between students and faculty is considered a partnership — the word "collegial" implies shared responsibility. Many professors use a method of teaching that requires students to discuss and answer questions posed by the instructor.

23. How can I communicate better with my professors?

Introduce yourself to establish an academic relationship. This will make it easier to raise questions and concerns about the class and assignments later. You can talk to your professor after class or during office hours, which should be in your syllabus. Note the professor's preferred method of communication, typically email, and use that to ask questions not answered during office hours. Include a relevant subject line and the class your question pertains to. Be direct and concise when writing emails to professors. Don't be afraid to ask a question twice, or for clarification if you do not understand a response.

24. Is it emotionally hard for American families to send their children away to college?

It depends on the family, and people in the same family don't always act the same way. Common reactions may range from sadness that the son or daughter is "leaving the nest" to pride for the accomplishment of pursuing higher education.

25. Is it financially hard for American families to send their children away to college?

It can be very challenging. Family income and savings are key factors in affording college. For some families, one or both parents' income covers tuition, fees, books, housing, food and other costs of college. For others, college is possible only with loans, grants and scholarships. It is becoming increasingly common for students to work through school to help pay expenses. These students might also apply for aid and loans.

26. How much do U.S. college students study?

The Association of American Colleges and Universities advises students to spend two hours studying for every hour of class time. That would mean 30 hours of studying per week for a course load of 15 credits. However, studies by the National Survey of Student Engagement have consistently found that full-time college students spend roughly one hour of studying for each hour of class time.

27. Why do Americans do so many group projects?

Group projects require people to work together. People can be more productive, driven and innovative as a group. Group projects also allow for assignments of greater difficulty and complexity. They will help students collaborate professionally after graduation, as most students will work in teams throughout their career. According to the National

Survey of Student Engagement, positive group experiences contribute to individual learning, retention and academic success.

28. How is copying or plagiarism defined in America?

Plagiarism is using someone else's language, ideas or other original material without crediting the source. This applies to texts published in print or online, to manuscripts, and to other work, including photos and drawing. Quoting or paraphrasing can prevent written plagiarism. Quoting is using another's statement word for word in quotation marks and crediting the creator. Paraphrasing is restating another's ideas in your own words without quotation marks. The original author should still be credited for the idea. Students who plagiarize can fail an assignment, an entire course or be expelled.

Race

29. Why is racism such an issue in America?

The United States has a complicated racial and ethnic history. It includes slavery of Native Americans and Africans; genocide and removal of Native Americans; the annexation of parts of Mexico that now make up several western states; the internment of Japanese Americans after Pearl Harbor and the civil rights struggle of African Americans. Arabs and other people of Middle Eastern descent experienced racism following the 2001 terrorist attacks. America still faces issues with workplace discrimination and stereotyping in popular culture.

30. Why is it that when Americans ask, "Where are you from?" they usually mean my race and not my country?

Race is a key identifier in the United States. Some people feel uneasy when they can't identify someone's race or ethnicity. Race, more than nationality, might give an American a set of preconceived notions of what someone might be like. When race is not obvious, it is called racial ambiguity. If questions about your national origin or race make you feel uncomfortable, you don't have to answer.

31. In cafeterias, people seem to prefer sitting with people of their racial group. Do people of different races mix?

People of different races do mix. However, sometimes people are more comfortable around others with similar social backgrounds and experiences. This is evident in "lunchroom situations." Many people are comfortable mingling with different races, though. According to Pew Research, most Americans under the age of 30 have friends of races other than their own and a vast majority approve of interracial dating. Try asking if you can sit with a group of people from another race. The worst that could happen is that they will say no.

32. Why do some Americans assume that I don't speak English because I look Asian and have black hair?

Asians and Asian Americans encounter this stereotype. The stereotype reflects a lack of knowledge or experience. Sometimes, people assume that an American is an international student based only on appearance. Correct the person who has been mistaken.

33. Why are American people so quick to stereotype other people?

Again, this has been a historic issue in America. People have been stereotyping since the country was created. Although most people are aware that stereotypes can be harmful, they exist. Exposure to wider groups of people and more conversation — the goal of this guide to cultural competence — can replace stereotypes with information and understanding.

Religion

34. Americans seem to have many religions. What are the main ones?

According to Pew Research, 78.4 percent of all adults in the United States call themselves Christians. That includes Protestants, Catholics, Mormons, Jehovah's Witnesses, Greek and Russian Orthodox and more. About 4.7 percent of Americans practice other religions such as Judaism, Buddhism, Islam and Hinduism. Sixteen percent of adults are unaffiliated and that proportion is growing among younger Americans.

35. Are Americans more religious than people in other countries?

A 2009 Gallup poll asked people around the world whether religion was part of their daily lives. About two-thirds of Americans said it was. That was about in the middle of the range of responses countries gave. A 2013 Gallup study showed that Americans say they feel religion is losing influence in the United States.

36. Why are Americans so fascinated with religion?

Constitutional protection of religious freedom and the large number of religions practiced in the United States make it interesting to many, but not all. Because religions are related to several other values, some people ask about religion to learn about someone quickly.

37. How do Americans find the time to practice their religion with their busy schedules?

Religions have different traditions that require varying amounts of time. People who practice the same religion might do it in different ways, adjusting schedules and their participation.

38. What are important religious holidays in the United States?

Because three-quarters of Americans are Christian, those holidays dominate. They include Christmas and Easter. Most Christians celebrate Christmas on Dec. 25. Eastern Orthodox Christians celebrate Christmas on Jan. 7. Easter falls in the spring, and its date moves. Major Jewish holidays are Yom Kippur, Rosh Hashanah and the weeklong Sukkot, and all have moving dates. The major Muslim holiday is Ramadan, a month-long observance that also moves and concludes with Eid-al-Fitr. Hindus celebrate Krishna Janmashtami. Several East Asian religions celebrate Diwali, and there are several dates for Asian new year festivals.

39. What are major non-religious holidays in America?

They include New Year's Day, Martin Luther King Jr. Day, Valentine's Day, Presidents' Day, St. Patrick's Day, Memorial Day, Independence Day, Labor Day, Columbus Day, Halloween, Veterans Day and Thanksgiving Day. U.S. businesses are not required to close on national holidays, as they are in some other countries.

Work and Money

40. How much do Americans work?

The United States, with an average of 1,798 hours worked per year, is seventh on CNNMoney's list of the hardest working countries in the world. The top six were Mexico (2,317), Chile (2,102), South Korea (2,092), Estonia (2,021), the Russian Federation (2,002) and Poland (1,893). Four out of five employed Americans work 35 or more hours a week.

41. Why don't Americans take more days off?

The United States is the only developed country without legally required paid vacation days or holidays. Austria and Portugal lead the world with 35 paid days off a year. The average U.S. worker receives 16 paid vacation days and holidays a year. One-fourth of Americans do not have any paid days off.

42. Why are a lot of Americans so willing to work overtime?

Overtime is a choice between time and money. Some workers don't have a choice about whether to work overtime. Some ask for it, and some avoid it. Overtime hours are often paid at "time and a half," which means 1 ½ times the rate paid for regular hours.

43. Is success at work important to Americans?

This varies according to the person and is related to job satisfaction. Good performance can also lead to raises and promotions. A Gallup Poll report in 2013 said that 29 percent of American workers said they felt engaged or inspired by their jobs. Worldwide, with 142 countries studied, the average was 13 percent.

44. How wealthy are people in the United States?

Income per person is around $30,000 a year, but it is distributed unequally. Including investments, property and other forms of wealth, the top 7 percent of U.S. households had a mean net worth of more than $3 million each in 2011, according to Pew Research. The mean for the other households was about $120,000. Many were much lower.

45. Do Americans save or spend?

A 2013 report from bankrate.com found that only 24 percent of Americans have enough money saved for at least six months, and half have less than three months' expenses saved. Twenty-seven percent had no emergency savings at all. A Gallup Poll in April 2013 showed that people with an annual income below $20,000 said they preferred saving over spending, 73 percent to 25 percent. People with annual incomes of $75,000 or more preferred saving by a ratio of 55 percent to 43 percent. According to the Organization for Economic Co-Operation and Development, the average American savings rate of 4 percent was about one-third of Spain's and one-half of the United Kingdom's.

46. At what age do Americans get jobs?

The nation's Fair Labor Standards Act sets 14 as the minimum age for employment and limits the number of hours that individuals under 16 can work. Jobs for 16-year-olds are typically limited to part-time, minimum-wage jobs, but hours in which they can work are not limited. Once people turn 18, they are not subject to restrictions on jobs or hours. Many parents encourage children to work to teach them independence. According to the U.S. Census Bureau, 25 percent of high school students have part-time jobs. Jobs for teens include retail, fast food, hospitality and lawn care.

47. How important is money to Americans?

Money is tied to "the pursuit of happiness," a value cited in the U.S. Declaration of Independence. In "United America," Wayne Baker says this is a core American value and that some people use money in pursuit of happiness. It doesn't always work. According to a 2013 Phillips Work/Life Survey, Americans prefer a job that is fulfilling over one with a higher salary that is less fulfilling. Seventy-nine percent of workers said they would be willing to take a salary cut for a job that allowed them to do more fulfilling work. Forty-three percent even said they would be willing to take a pay cut of 25 percent or more.

Culture

48. Do Americans travel to see their country and the world?

According to the U.S. Travel Association, Americans spent 2 billion nights more than 50 miles from home for business or pleasure in 2012. Top reasons for pleasure travel were to visit relatives or friends, shop, dine or go to the beach. According to the U.S. State Department, about 39 percent of Americans now have passports. The World Tourism Organization reports that U.S. travelers spend more money overseas than people from any other country, and the United States is one of the biggest beneficiaries of spending from other countries.

49. It seems like Americans care a lot about sports. Do they?

According to journalist Amanda Ripley, "When I surveyed about 200 former exchange students … in cooperation with an international exchange organization called AFS, nine out of 10 foreign students who had lived in the United States said that kids here cared more about sports than their peers back home did. A majority of Americans who'd studied abroad agreed."

50. Why do Americans cheer at football and basketball games?

Sports are extremely popular in America. Some games attract 100,000 fans in person, and are broadcast to millions. Sports are a way to be connected to a team. Fans participate by cheering, and some coaches say this helps teams win.

51. Why do some Americans spend a lot of time at the mall?

For some, looking at merchandise is recreation. They might not even buy anything. Also, shopping malls are designed to be community centers so they can attract people to spend time there, shop, eat at restaurants and get services such as haircuts. Some even have play areas for children or work-out centers. Citizens use malls for exercise walking in bad weather. In many U.S. cities, malls have replaced once busy downtown shopping areas.

52. Do Americans constantly need to spend money or be entertained?

According to the U.S. Bureau of Labor Statistics, the average American family spent $51,442 in 2012, and $2,605 of that was spent on entertainment. Another $2,678 was spent on food eaten away from home. In its American Time Use Survey, the bureau reports that Americans spend about five hours a day being entertained. Television accounted for 2.8 hours of that time followed by socializing and communicating at 37 minutes and 28 minutes playing games.

Health

53. How good is the U.S. health care system?

The health care system changed significantly in October 2013 with the adoption of the Affordable Care Act, so this picture might change. Two months earlier, Bloomberg.com rated the United States health care system as the world's most expensive and least effective.

54. Why do Americans care so much about being in shape?

According the U.S. Centers for Disease Control and Prevention, two of 10 adult Americans get the recommended levels of exercise needed. More than a quarter of Americans do not spend any time exercising.

55. Do Americans care about their health?

Many Americans care about their health. According to Forbes Magazine, America ranked 11th out of 15 on the list of healthiest countries. The average life expectancy in the United States is 81 for women and 79 for men, for a ranking of about 35th in the world. The top countries are about four years higher. On infant mortality, another measure of health, the United States has not improved as much in recent years as other advanced nations.

56. Why is the legal drinking age 21? I know many Americans under 21 who drink.

The U.S. Centers for Disease Control and Prevention calls alcohol use by people under 21 a major health problem. However, the underage drinking rate has been declining in the U.S. The 2012 Monitoring the Future Study reported "continuing decreases in alcohol consumption among students in 8th, 10th, and 12th grades." A 2012 study by the University of Michigan reported that, compared to 36 European countries, the United States had the second-lowest proportion of students who use tobacco and alcohol.

57. Why do you have to be 18 years old to buy cigarettes?

For health reasons. While a few countries allow people as young as 16 to buy cigarettes, 46 of the 50 states, most of the European Union and most other countries have set 18 as the minimum age for purchasing cigarettes.

58. If marijuana is illegal, why do so many people smoke it?

For years, there has been a movement across the United States to decriminalize marijuana. Laws and penalties have been relaxed. Studies by Pew and Gallup said that in 2013, for the first time, most Americans favor legalization.

59. Do Americans drink a lot of coffee?

Coffee is an important part of American life. According to a National Coffee Association study in 2013, 83 percent of American adults drink coffee, the highest proportion in the world. Sixty-three percent of respondents said they drink coffee every day. The daily drinker has an average of three cups. Another group, the International Coffee Organization, said Brazil had the second-most coffee drinkers and Germany was third.

60. Do Americans appreciate a clean environment?

In a 2013 HuffPost/YouGov poll, 39 percent of respondents said the environment was very important, 41 percent said it was fairly important and 16 percent said it was not too important. This was down from a poll conducted 40 years earlier, around the time the United States created the Environmental Protection Agency.

61. Why are there so many guns in the United States?

The U.S. Constitution's Second Amendment protects gun ownership. There are frequent debates about whether there should be restrictions on gun ownership and each debate seems to prompt a surge in gun sales. America has about 270 million guns, or about 89 for every 100 people. The second-place country in guns per person is Yemen, with about 55 per 100 people. Many Americans own more than one gun and the proportion of gun owners has been declining. A University of Chicago study showed that gun ownership declined from 54 percent in 1977 to 32 percent in 2010.

62. Do Americans spend a lot of time outdoors?

A 2013 report by The Outdoor Foundation estimated that 141.9 million Americans participated in an average of 87 outings in 2012. The most frequent activities were running, bicycling, fishing, camping and hiking. People pay taxes and fees to support local, state and federal parks and bike paths.

63. Why are American men so tall?

Major factors in height are genetics, diet and health care. The average height of men in the United States is 5 feet, 10 inches (1.8 meters). The average height for American women is 5 feet, 4 ½ inches (1.6 meters). Twenty-five to 30 countries have taller average heights than the United States.

Food

64. Why do Americans eat so quickly?

Some Americans do eat fast. According to the U.S. Department of Agriculture, Americans 15 and older spend 67 minutes per day mainly eating or drinking. An additional 23.5 minutes are spent eating while doing something else, and 63 minutes are spent drinking beverages while doing something else. Statistics show that the faster you eat, the more calories you take in before you're full. What is true for one person or even most people is not true for everyone.

65. How often do Americans eat?

The American standard is having three meals a day: breakfast, lunch and dinner. However, many Americans also snack between meals and eat dessert after their meals. Americans eat on different schedules.

66. Why are the meal portions so large?

Many Americans eat large portions at a meal. Much of that has to do with plate size. CBS News research shows that 54 percent of Americans will eat until their plate is clean. And plates have been getting larger. As the portion size goes up, so can appetite, as the large plate tricks you into thinking you're still hungry. Americans who want to control their portions usually eat off a smaller plate — something around seven to nine inches.

67. Why do Americans eat unhealthy food?

According to U.S. News & World Report, processed foods contain an abundance of salt, sugar and saturated fat. In Gallup's 2013 Consumption Poll, 80 percent of Americans said they eat at fast-food restaurants at least once a month.

Almost half said they eat fast food at least once a week. For "Salt Sugar Fat: How the Food Giants Hooked Us," New York Times reporter Michael Moss interviewed more than 300 people in the processed food industry. He concluded, "What I found, over four years of research and reporting, was a conscious effort — taking place in labs and marketing meetings and grocery-store aisles — to get people hooked on foods that are convenient and inexpensive."

68. Why do American restaurants operate so quickly?

Generally, the restaurants that operate quickly are low-priced, with the intention of getting their customers in and out. However, fancier restaurants tend to operate much slower. These restaurants are designed for customers who aren't in a hurry and don't mind spending more money on their meal than at a fast-food establishment.

69. Why are some Americans vegetarian?

Research shows that 3.2 percent of American adults, or 7.3 million people, follow a vegetarian-based diet. There are a variety of reasons for this. Some people want to live longer, healthier lives, while others have always loved animals and are ethically opposed to eating them. According to Vegetarianism in America, a low-in-fat vegetarian diet can assist in keeping your weight down, as well as help in preventing disease caused from the fat and cholesterol in meats.

70. Do American families have certain traditions for eating meals?

The CBS News poll "Where America Stands" reported that 74 percent of families said they eat together on most weekdays. The Journal of American Medicine reported a much lower figure of 43 percent. Both numbers were up from a 2003 Gallup Poll estimate that 28 percent of adults with children under 18 are at home together seven nights a week. That number in 1997 was 37 percent.

71. Why are organic options and healthy choices so scarce in grocery stores?

The availability of organic food is dependent on two things: location and cost. Organic food is still more expensive than non-organic food in the United States, and while it is becoming more available in standard grocery stores, wide selections might still be confined to areas with stores that specialize in organic food.

72. Pop, soda or Coke?

Carbonated soft drinks go by all these names. The difference is regional. Pop is the dominant term in most northern states. Soda is preferred in New England, California, Nevada, Arizona and around Missouri. Coke, which has its headquarters in Atlanta, is used in the South to refer to any carbonated soft drink. Ask Americans from different places about their preference.

73. How common is obesity in America?

According the U.S. Centers for Disease Control and Prevention, more than a third of U.S. adults are obese. The rate for children and adolescents is 17 percent, three times the rate a generation ago. The United States led the world in obesity until Mexico passed it in 2013.

Family

74. Are family members in America close?

The American family is changing. The number of families with children from more than one marriage is growing, more gay couples are parents, and there are more families in which the parents are not married. Families with more than two adult generations under the same roof have been growing since 1970. Immigrants drive much of the move toward traditional families. A weak economy and later marriages has meant that more adult children live with their parents.

75. How much time do Americans spend with their families?

It is hard to find a number for this, but some trends are worth noting. People are living longer with their parents and getting married later. Women are spending more hours working and men are spending more time with household business. The Internet is taking a bigger share of people's time. Some trends imply more family time, some mean less.

76. Why is every person in a family treated like an individual?

American families tend to be both individualistic and collective. While family members have their own identity, thoughts and opinions, they understand that they are part of something larger. The idea that the "sum is greater than its parts" can be applied to American families. Family members are allowed to work to achieve their goals and be independent, in most cases, although they do not traditionally believe that they are more important than the family.

77. Why doesn't everyone in a family have to share everything?

The level of sharing is different in each family. It is common for family members to share small everyday items like food and household necessities. In some cases, children share bedrooms and even vehicles. It is also common for siblings to share clothing. Family members generally do not share personal items such as toiletries. It is thought that certain items are appropriate to share and more intimate items are for personal use only.

78. Why do children have to do chores?

Parents have children do household chores to help the family and to teach responsibility. Examples of chores could include unloading the dishwasher, making the bed, cleaning the bathroom, clearing the dinner table or taking out the trash. A time-use study at the University of Maryland said U.S. children do chores for fewer than three hours per week.

79. Why is it the norm for children to move out of the house before marriage?

Adult children are expected to become self-sufficient and to live on their own. This depends on them being able to support themselves. U.S. Census data shows that this is happening later. From 2007 to the spring of 2011, the number of adults aged 25-34 living in their parents' household rose from 4.7 million to 5.9 million, an increase for that age group from 11.8 percent to 14.2 percent. This was attributed to the weak economy.

80. Are Americans pressured by their families to marry young?

The average first-marriage age for women is 26. This is older than it is for most countries and is similar to the marriage age in Canada, Romania, Greece, Chile and The Bahamas.

For U.S. men, the age is 28. Both averages have been rising since 1970. This occurs for many reasons: More people are having children before getting married, it is now more common for people to live together before marriage, and as education rates for women rise, more women delay marriage longer.

81. How common is divorce in America?

America's divorce rate has been declining, but is still high compared to rates in other countries. One way to compare countries is by the number of divorces as a percentage of marriages. The U.S. rate was 45 percent in 2011. Around that time, Sweden, Belarus, Finland and Luxembourg had higher rates. The U.S. rate was about the same as Estonia, Australia, Denmark and Belgium.

82. How old are Americans when they start to drive?

Driving laws vary by state, and many have restrictions for young drivers. The legal driving age is generally 16, one of the lowest in the world. Some states offer provisional or hardship licenses as early as age 14. In recent years, fewer than half of teens have been getting their licenses within the first year they are eligible. They wait for financial reasons, to avoid restrictions, for safety and for a lack of interest.

83. Do Americans respect parents and elders?

This varies widely. According to the Pew Research Center, those of the Millennial generation (18- to 29-year-olds) respect their elders more than previous generations. Sixty percent of Millennials feel that they should let an aging parent move in with them and care for them if that is what the parent prefers. In comparison, fewer than 40 percent of Americans 60 and older feel that this is their responsibility.

Relationships

84. What does it mean when Americans hug friends or acquaintances?

Hugging between Americans can be interpreted as a sign of affection, friendship or even a greeting. It is more common to hug friends than to hug someone you just met. However, some Americans have a tendency to be friendlier upon meeting people and it is not unheard of or socially unacceptable to hug an acquaintance. You are not expected to hug your friends or someone you just met. It is completely based on how comfortable you feel around the person.

85. Are Americans from different areas of the country the same?

No. Americans have regional interests, mannerisms and body language. For example, Americans in major cities such as New York City are said to be a bit more "pushy" or aggressive and always in a hurry, while Americans who live in the Midwest are seen as more polite and friendly to strangers. Regional differences can also be reflected in preferences for food and activities.

86. How sexually active are Americans?

The average age for first-time sex is 17, according to the Guttmacher Institute. By the time Americans are 19, 71 percent have had sex. Men have sex at slightly younger ages. The frequency of sex varies according to a number of factors, especially age and the length of the relationship. According to the Kinsey Institute, 18- to 29-year-olds have sex an average of 112 times a year. People in their 30s average 86 times per year and people in their 40s average 69 times a year.

87. Americans talk openly about sexual experiences, even around strangers. Why?

Some people brag about their sexual activity to increase their social standing. There is a double standard in how people are judged for this. While it may enhance a man's reputation among friends, it can hurt a woman's reputation. There are also ongoing national discussions about sexual freedom.

88. Do Americans show their affection in public?

Yes, they do. However, how much they display depends on the couple. In a lot of cases you'll see hand-holding, hugs or quick kisses on the cheeks or lips. Some take it further, though.

89. What does it mean to go on a date?

To go on a date means to spend time alone with someone you are romantically interested in. The goal is to get to know each other better.

90. How do I ask someone out on a date?

Typically, Americans get to know someone before they ask for a date. This can mean talking in a social setting several times. They might discuss shared interests, opinions and values. When one of them is interested and feels the other might be, too, that person suggests an activity they could do together.

91. What does a date include?

Dating is very casual and informal in the United States. People spend time together and don't even need to call it a date. Socially, a date can be anything you both want to do. It could mean dinner, an event or entertainment, or just a walk to get ice cream. People can also get to know each other in larger groups where no one is paired off with anyone else.

92. Does dating mean having sex?

It can, but only if both people agree. If someone forces sex on another person who is not willing or who is unable to freely consent, it is a crime in the United States. It is safest and most respectful to not pressure someone to do something they do not want to do. If you aren't sure whether the other person is willing, don't have sex with them. If you are assaulted, call the police.

Language

93. What is the easiest way to learn English in America?

There are many tools to help people learn English. Videos, books, online lessons and classroom lessons can help. The easiest way, though, is to speak English as much as possible and talk with native speakers.

94. Why are there English words that sound the same but have different meanings?

This is one thing that makes English difficult. Words that sound alike but have different meanings are called homonyms. Examples include "weather" and "whether" or "plain" and "plane." Long before it came to America, English developed out of words and rules borrowed from several other languages.

95. Why do most Americans speak only English?

Although America does not have an official language, English is the primary language and can be used in most situations. In many countries, colonization meant that one language was imposed on another and multilingualism became widespread. Most parts of the United States were developed in ways that kept only English.

96. Americans speak English with many different accents. Why is that the case?

Because the United States is so large, there are many different regions. Often, people in one area speak English differently than those in another place. The ethnic composition, lifestyle, culture and location of a region influence the way English is spoken there.

97. Is personal privacy important to Americans?

Yes. The Bill of Rights reflects Americans' concern for personal privacy. The First Amendment protects the right to believe and speak as one wishes, the Third Amendment protects the privacy of the home against demands, the Fourth Amendment protects against unreasonable searches and the Fifth Amendment protects people in court from revealing information that could be used against them.

98. Why do Americans always say what is on their mind?

The First Amendment protects freedom of speech and American society encourages people to speak their mind about everything, including what they see as injustices or mistakes.

99. How would you describe American humor?

American humor can be hard to understand. It often focuses on everyday situations and might include cultural references that require some background understanding. American humor can be less subtle and more physical than humor in other countries.

100. How can I learn American slang?

American slang is not easy to learn. Slang is always changing and terms might not have obvious meanings. There is a guide in the back of this book to help you learn some of these terms and a couple of websites to help you keep up.

Slang and Idioms

AMERICAN ENGLISH HAS expressions that require some explanation. They can seem odd or unclear the first time you hear them.

ASAP: This is the abbreviation, or quick way of saying, "As soon as possible."

Awesome: This means cool, fantastic or amazing. It often expresses admiration or approval.

Baby boomer or boomer: Someone born in the Baby Boom between 1946 and 1964 when the U.S. birth rate drastically increased.

Badass: Really good or cool. It can mean something is a little dangerous or menacing.

Bar crawl or pub crawl: A night during which friends go to many bars. Many American students have a "bar crawl" for their 21st birthday, the first time they can legally drink alcohol.

Bar star: Someone who frequents bars and consumes large amounts of alcohol.

Beat a dead horse: Repetitious talk about a situation or decision that is not going to change.

BFF/bestie: Best friend forever or closest friend.

Bro: Short for brother. A man's male friend.

Butterflies in my stomach: Nervousness, such as a fluttering feeling in the stomach from anxiety or excitement.

Chick flick / chick lit: Movies or literature stereotypically favored by women. These often have a romantic plot.

Creeping: Looking someone up on social media networks. Finding someone on Facebook, Twitter or through Google without following them or sending them a friend request.

Doggie bag: A restaurant provides one of these for leftover food that is to be taken home. More commonly, diners ask for a box to carry leftovers.

Down with that: Agreement or consent. Someone may agree with a suggestion by saying "I'm down with that" or simply, "I'm down."

Dub (W): The letter "W," pronounced "double-you," is shortened to dub. Someone might say "by the way" as "btw" or "bt-dubs." The restaurant chain Buffalo Wild Wings is called "B-Dubs."

For here, or to go? Fast-food workers ask this to determine whether they should put your meal on a tray for eating in the restaurant, or in a bag for you to take it elsewhere.

FYI: "For your information." Usually needs no reply.

Hipster: Someone outside the cultural mainstream who is counter-culture, progressive and typically likes art, films and indie rock.

Hooking up: This is usually sexual and can be deliberately vague. It might mean anything from kissing to having sex. It can also mean doing a favor for someone: "Can you hook me up with a ride?"

Hot mess: Describes someone who is struggling or having a difficult time. Can be humorous or derogatory. "I'm a hot mess today."

How's it going? A greeting like "hello." No detailed response is expected.

(I'll) see you later: Doesn't literally mean seeing someone later, or even anytime soon. It means goodbye.

It is what it is: Expresses acceptance or resignation to circumstances. Used when there seems to be no alternative or solution.

OCD: Obsessive Compulsive Disorder, a psychological disorder. Many Americans use it casually to refer to obsessive behavior.

Plan B: An alternate plan, or a different solution. Can also refer to birth control.

Piece of cake: An easy task.

Raining cats and dogs: Heavy rain.

RSVP: From the French "répondez, s'il vous plaît." This means "please reply" and is usually part of an invitation. If an invitation says RSVP, you are expected to say whether you can come.

Small talk: Conversation that is brief and casual. Topics are broad and not serious. People make small talk with new acquaintances.

Stalking (on social media): See creeping.

Status quo: The way things are, especially in terms of work, society or politics.

Staying on top of it: To stay informed or in control of a situation.

Tailgating: Parking and opening the back of one's car and having a small party with friends and family before a sporting event. Tailgates often include food and alcohol.

TBA: "To be announced." This often means that an important detail, such as when an event will occur, will come later. TBD means "to be determined."

The way to the heart is through the stomach: This type of saying is called a proverb. There are many others. This one comes from England and means that good cooking can win someone's love.

This is my jam: Used to identify one's favorite song as it is played on the radio or in a social setting.

To AP out: Testing out of a college course. Advanced Placement courses in high school end with national exams where high scores allow some students to skip introductory college courses.

To rock (an item): Most often used for clothing. "I'm going to rock this dress tonight."

Train wreck: This is rarely used to describe an actual train crash or accident, but rather to describe a disastrous situation, event or person. "He's a train wreck." (See hot mess.)

Umbrella drink: An alcoholic drink with a small paper umbrella. These beverages are often tropical drinks that are sweet and frozen or blended. Sometimes they are associated with vacations or relaxation. Examples include piña coladas and daiquiris.

Y'all: Americans from the southern United States use this to address two or more people. It means "you all." When there are more people, a person might say, "all y'all."

Wing it: Making it up as you go, improvising. Someone who has not prepared for a presentation might just "wing it."

Texting Expressions

BRB: Be right back
BRT: Be right there
BTW: By the way
IDC: I don't care
IDK: I don't know
IMHO: In my humble opinion
LMAO: Laughing my ass off
LOL: Laugh out loud
MEH: Not impressed
NP: No problem
NVM: Never mind
OMG: Oh my god!
UOK: Are you OK?
WBY: What about you?

Resources

Books

Baker, Wayne. *United America: The Surprising Truth About American Values, American Identity and the 10 Beliefs That a Large Majority of Americans Holds* Dear. Canton, Mich.: Read the Spirit Books, 2013.

The College Board. *International Student Handbook of U.S. Colleges*, 26th ed. The College Board, 2012.

Dervaes, Claudine, and John Hunter. *The UK to USA Dictionary: British English vs. American English*, 3rd ed. Inverness, Fl.: Solitaire Publishing, 2012.

Matllns, Stuart M., and Arthur Magida. *How to Be a Perfect Stranger: The Essential Religious Etiquette Handbook*, 5th ed. Woodstock, Vt.: Skylight Paths Publishing, 2010.

Stewart, Edward C., and Milton J Bennett. *American Cultural Patterns: A Cross-Cultural Perspective*, 2nd ed. Boston: Nicholas Brealey Publishing, 2005

Takaki, Ronald. *A Different Mirror: A History of Multicultural America*, revised. New York: Back Bay Books, 2008.

Websites

Eight Campus Resources for International Students from U.S. News & World Report: http://www.usnews.com/education/best-colleges/articles/2011/12/08/8-campus-resources-for-international-students

Ediplomat: United States cultural etiquette: http://www.ediplomat.com/np/cultural_etiquette/ce_us.htm

Guide to U.S. by an international student: http://redbus2us.com/ (http://redbus2us.com/)

Immihelp: http://www.immihelp.com/

Online Slang Dictionary: http://onlineslangdictionary.com/

Study in the US: http://www.internationalstudentguidetothe-usa.com

Studying in the United States, U.S. News & World Report: http://www.usnews.com/education/best-colleges/studying-in-the-united-states

Travel Facts & Statistics: http://www.ustravel.org/news/press-kit/travel-facts-and-statistics

Urban Dictionary: (http://www.urbandictionary.com/)

U.S. Higher Education Glossary: http://www.usnews.com/education/best-colleges/articles/2011/08/15/us-higher-education-glossary

Organizations

NAFSA: Association of International Educators
1307 New York Avenue NW, 8th Floor,
Washington, DC 20005-4701
http://www.nafsa.org/

Institute of International Education
http://www.iie.org/

Also in This Series

100 Questions and Answers About Indian Americans
Coming soon:
100 Questions and Answers About Arab Americans
100 Questions, 500 Nations (Native Americans)
100 Questions and Answers About Hispanics and Latinos

For Copies

Copies of this guide in paperback or ebook formats may be ordered from Amazon.

For a volume discount on copies or a special edition customized and branded for your university or organization, contact David Crumm Media, LLC at info@DavidCrummMedia.com.

For more information and further discussion visit: http://nws.jrn.msu.edu/culturalcompetence/ (http://nws.jrn.msu.edu/culturalcompetence/)

Lightning Source UK Ltd.
Milton Keynes UK
UKOW05f1606120717
305175UK00002B/582/P